OHIO BLUE TIPS

AKRON SERIES IN POETRY

Ohio Blue Tips was published with the support of
a grant from the Greenwall Fund of The Academy
of American Poets.

Winner of the 1997 Akron Poetry Prize

AKRON SERIES IN POETRY

Elton Glaser, Editor

Barry Seiler, *The Waters of Forgetting*

Raeburn Miller, *The Comma After Love: Selected Poems of Raeburn Miller*

William Greenway, *How the Dead Bury the Dead*

Jon Davis, *Scrimmage of Appetite*

Anita Feng, *Internal Strategies*

Susan Yuzna, *Her Slender Dress*

Raeburn Miller, *The Collected Poems of Raeburn Miller*

Clare Rossini, *Winter Morning with Crow*

Barry Seiler, *Black Leaf*

William Greenway, *Simmer Dim*

Jeanne E. Clark, *Ohio Blue Tips*

OHIO BLUE TIPS

Jeanne E. Clark

THE UNIVERSITY OF AKRON PRESS

AKRON, OHIO

PS
3553
.L28573
O35
1999

Acknowledgments:

My thanks to the editors of the following magazines, in which some of these poems previously appeared, a few in different versions: *Blue Mesa Review, Calliope, 5 AM, Michigan Quarterly Review, The Midwest Quarterly, 1995 National Poetry Competition Anthology, Ohio Poetry Review, One Meadway, The Oxford Magazine, Parting Gifts, Pleaides, Quarterly West, Tucson Guide Quarterly, Visions-International, Weber Studies,* and *Willow Springs.*

"Joe Silver," "The House Next Door," "Prison School," and "Reckoning" also appear in different versions in *Tumblewords: Writers Reading the West* (Reno: University of Nevada Press, 1995).

"Tractors" and "On the Day before Joe Silver Was Made" also appear in different versions in *Fever Dreams: Contemporary Arizona Poetry* (Tucson: University of Arizona Press, 1997).

"This Summer That Isn't Mine" was awarded the 1995 Loft Prize in Poetry.

Heartfelt thanks to Theresa Hannon and Laura Lee Washburn for line by line ministrations, and to Karla, Diann, Denis, and Roberta for sitting where I can always see you. Thank you, David Lee, for baling wire on and off the page.

All inquiries and permissions requests should be addressed to the Publisher, The University of Akron Press, 374B Bierce Library, Akron, Ohio 44325-1703.

Library of Congress Cataloging-in-Publication Data

Clark, Jeanne E., 1954–
    Ohio blue tips : a book of poems / by Jeanne E. Clark.
        p.   cm. — (Akron series in poetry)
    ISBN 1-884836-43-7 (cloth). — ISBN 1-884836-44-5 (pbk.)
    1. Farm life—Ohio—Poetry. I. Title. II. Series.
    PS3553.L28573O35 1999
    811'.54—dc21   98-51955
                                                                              CIP

Manufactured in the United States of America
First Edition
The paper used in this publication meets the minimum requirements of American National Standard for Information Sciences—Permanence of Paper for Printed Library Materials, ANSI z39.48-1984. ⊗

for my darling

for my son

Contents

III

I am the place in which something has occurred.

—*Claude Levi-Strauss*

I

Reckoning

The Man said, he's dangerous, Miss.
And Joe smiled,
A yellow-toothed smile, chicken fat yellow.
The Man said, if I take these cuffs off him . . .
And I said, take them off.
When Joe put his two uncuffed hands on my shoulders,
He was laughing like something was really funny,
With the Man saying, he ain't like a human being.
And me saying, what's wrong with him,
And wondering what Joe—now dangerous
Because some woman the state paid
$200 a month to raise him
Kept him seven years in a chicken coop—
What was Joe going to do next?
I'm going to put those cuffs back on,
The Man said, before we all live to regret it.

Quinn Margaret's Mother Speaks Her Mind

What've you got
To show for yourself?
My mother says, Quinn Margaret,
You've got a job
That underplays your potential—
Teaching criminals
And retardeds their numbers.
For a smart kid,
That's pretty dumb.
And don't think for a minute
I forgot.
That boy of yours
With his name
Like a wild west show,
A name
That's neither family
Nor Bible,
Jack Wyatt, you should know
Drops his pencils on the floor.
His teacher says
You've got to spend time
Every day
With a boy like that.
Well, I say,
Get Jesus in his heart
And get a Kleenex
For his nose.
First time I saw him
In that picture from the wedding,
I said, that boy's a runner.
He's got his father's nose.
I said, she'll have to chase after

The two of them.
And you did, didn't you?

Quinn, you should put it all behind you.
Then again, I remember
How stubborn you were.
It started,
You know,
In the third grade.
You remember I told you
What the teacher said,
Nowadays it's the sixties,
And lefthanders don't write
With a hook.
She corrected you
Time and again.
And to this day,
I don't know where you get it,
You won't write cursive.
You make your letters
Straight like a typewriter's
Up-and-down print.
Well, you can't fool me.
I can read between the lines.
I know you're really
Just like your father,
Backslidden and given over
To a reprobate mind.

Sometimes I just don't know
What I'm praying for,
What kind of trouble you're in—
A woman at the home
Where I work
Says her daughter says
You're seeing a man with a past.
She says he's a fire-setter,

That he's got a tattoo
On the low part of his arm,
That at a work picnic
He rolled up his sleeves.
He didn't care who could see.
My friend's daughter says
She's seen you with him
Under the water tower
In the field
Behind the State Hospital.
She's seen you. Quinn Margaret,
The Lord says right in the Bible,
Isaiah 3:16,
That just like you
The daughters of Zion walked
With their haughty necks outstretched
Just like they were something.
Their eyes, he says,
Were glancing and wanton.
And Miss-Don't-Listen-To-Anyone,
The Lord God, he smote them
With a scab, do you hear?
And he laid bare
All their secret parts.
Honey, all I'm saying is
I'm afraid for you.

Prison School

I graded papers in the afternoons.
The table was four-by-nine, inmate-built.
They only stayed through the morning.

Today the school ward door opened. Henry Purdue,
The principal, talking to someone,
The sound of feet, fast and hard, down the hall,

My name backwards, NeeGee, not Jeanne E.,
Joe Silver, breathless, at the top of the steps,
His fatboy arms full of lilacs, gray T-shirt,

Chinos, the wet blue sneakers closed with Velcro.
He had been fishing, he said, for the first time.
Joe Silver threw the lilac branches down.

I asked him how he liked it. Joe Silver said
The lilacs were for me. These lilacs were,
Joe said, the only living things he could catch.

On His Sixteenth Birthday,
His Mother Calls the Season

Today is fall and revved-up
Engines with the brakes pushed to the floor.
Let up every now and then, you know,
How you want to move.
My grandmother said, every time she saw me,
What a headful of hair you have,
I could take a brush . . .
Your father's hands in my hair. The damn dog
Barking shrill. I'm high-strung,
Today, going nowhere.

Jack Wyatt, that boy back then didn't go to church,
But he played up to my mother,
Helping her with things, putting
His arms around her to say good-bye.
He called her Mom. One Christmas,
He kissed her on the lips.

He's sixteen, in a pile of leaves.
Schoonover Park. He's big,
A year older with a beard and on top of me.
The gardener, a slight man, rakes
The leaves into piles. He watches,
That slow turn of his head and then down.
He's thinking maybe about a daughter
My age. This isn't my first time.

Engine grease, what a boy smells like:
Leaves. He tastes like metal.
I couldn't tell at first, his lips
Thick and soft. What do I care?
I like that it's mine.

Joe Silver

Joe Silver, whose face is a flatiron
Whose face is thick yellow milk
Schoolroom paste hardened on a bristle brush
Whose walk is the strike down an alley
That makes a pinsetter jump
Whose walk is a schoolyard seesaw
Whose voice is the frozen lake breaking
Under December's first skaters
Joe Silver again whose teeth are the rap of knuckles against a door
Whose teeth are pegs in the joints of fine furniture
Whose mouth is a locked closet
Lipper on the deck of a whaler
Whose words walk backward out a door
Whose words are grayed laundry
Whose thoughts are the felt of a chalkboard eraser
Whose thoughts are a rolled-up newspaper
Whose head is hard water under a speedboat
Joe Silver, whose head is the egg of a Mute Swan
Whose hair is the sharp spine on a bluegill's back
Whose hair is the morning grass of the governor's front lawn
Whose eyes are the blue tips of kitchen matches
Whose eyes are boiled onions
Whose eyes are the split galls of a felled oak
Whose hands are charged with powder
Whose hands are a bluegown's tin cup
Birds full of buckshot jerking in midair

The House Next Door

The woman called you stupid, and stupid
Left the front porch door to her house

Open just a crack. The word *stupid* ran,
Bad child, in and out of that door.

The paperboy delivered the news
On the front lawn of the woman's house.

And with your fingers smeared black,
You pushed the paper,

Now burning, through the door
Because the woman called you stupid.

You set the morning on fire.
Bad child black hands morning woman next

Door crack stupid. You tried to tell them.
What happens next, you ask me,

When I tell you the story of the house next door.
They move you, I say, to a new house.

The Game Joe Silver Plays Alone and in the Dark

Joe Silver forgotten, but born,
Born in Ohio, born retarded,

Whole family of retardeds,
Aunts and uncles who took Joe Silver in.

Joe, born in the dark,
Away now from his family,

Away from his retarded house.
Joe is alone now in the dark,

Playing the dark
Retarded and alone,

The dark without parents or house.
Joe's playing is music.

It circles the outside of his head.
Music flying around Joe's head is a halo,

Smoke and gold leaf,
Gold leaves playing and falling in Joe's darkness.

Gold leaves are fall in Ohio,
Its smokestacks and children with sticks,

Sticks that roast marshmallows,
Smoke rising from the fire.

This darkness is the night
Where Joe plays with sticks in his hands,

This night with gold leaves
And smoke the burnt color of marshmallows,

Black with the gooey center
That tastes good when Joe remembers.

Joe playing alone without sound
Hears that damn music around his head,

The sizzle and pop marshmallows make in a fire.
Joe plays this game in the dark, forgets to wear clothes

Except for the light coming off his shoulders,
Creeping like some rich ferret,

Its sneak and silver Joe feels inside.
And the sky at night is lit up,

Glow-in-the-dark yo-yo Joe held in his hands,
That Joe held one day

When he was a kid in some other town
And played, dressed in get-dirty clothes.

Now his skin glows fluorescent,
That halo ferret on the shoulder,

Ferret dancing to some itchy music it must feel
In his body. And Joe feels the music, too,

Picks up two sticks, sits with them
In his hands like Buddha

Or something else that Joe knows nothing about.
He can feel the play in his body

Like smoke rising over Ohio,
Like marshmallow skin popping on the end of a stick.

Joe feels the play as he sits in the dark,
Naked with his fingers and toes,

Counting them: one, two, three.
Joe alone in the dark over and over

Starts this game with the sticks to music:
The music Joe hears inside his shoulders,

The music playing in Joe's legs and hands and the soft place
        between.
Joe plays this game alone in the dark

Again and again because he has this time,
His body and the music.

Joe forgotten is born now
Without anyone to see or to hear

Except a glow-in-the-dark sky
With smoke that is Ohio.

Time-Life Sends a Photojournalist

I don't want to say anything
Into that microphone, their stories
Protected by the laws of the state of Ohio.
You'll have to take your pictures without me.
The men in this block are retarded. They don't know
How they got here. The smart cons
All have stories, all of them framed,
A woman, best friend, a brother.
Evenings after work, I help the slow ones:
They killed fifteen men.
They burned down the junior high school
While the principal was in church. Their families
Turned out for the trial. You know,
After a story they sleep better.

I get letters all the time. One today said, I got
A doctor of divinity degree and $25,
Please, honey, let's get married. Another day,
A retarded man, Joe, brought me
An armload of lilacs. He had been fishing.
He said this was what he caught.

I have a boy, eleven years old. We moved
Back into my mother's house.
She keeps notarized copies,
John Dillinger's mug shots
And fingerprints in a kitchen drawer
Next to the silverware. Dillinger,
The most famous man my mother knew.
She worked the desk the day
He shot his way out of the courthouse.

My hometown is famous for that day,
The man Dillinger killed being his first.

The summer after my husband left,
I met a man from New York.
I took time off. We went sailing,
St. Mary's Lake. Here's a picture.

I think about quitting, going back to school.
The prison's gone crazy. Last winter,
An inmate got out. He followed me.
I can't take much more. My mother asks me
What will I do with my boy?
You think I could write
The captions for these pictures?

A Day for Fishing

A day that wouldn't begin, that overslept
In a Marlowe bed while others showered,
That shut its eyes again to daylight,
That slipped through window bars
Like slim fingers and along cement walls
Plastered with those pictures of naked ladies.
A day for fishing that after breakfast
Tucked in its gray pants and shirt.

A day that sat beside the quarry, that like limestone
And sadness wouldn't talk to other fishermen,
That didn't know how to smoke or sing Motown,
That removed its boots and entered the water
Swinging out hands and arms and thick head,
That forgetting hook and worm fished like a bear
Swimming belly up, in its way of falling.

On the Day before Joe Silver Was Made,
There Was a Train Engine out of Control

I go to meet the train and the train comes to meet me,
Embracing me as if I'm returning, as if I'm saying good-bye.

The train's deep sighs enter a mountain.
We come out on the other side the same.

Two trains: a black chicken,
A black cat without shadow.

The train is the body of Joe Silver
Without hope of resurrection. Car after car, it multiplies.

The train's conductor is blind, revealing
Destinations and Joe Silver's dumb cargo.

Who *is* Joe Silver that comes out of the wilderness
Like pillars of smoke with all the power of love?

Who *is* this barren chariot?
Joe Silver's bed ready for war.

Plains and grasslands, farms of Ohio, tell me:
Has the train I want come this way?

Train after train, travel's endless recurrence.
It's a lie to say I never wanted to board.

A train wreck, Joe Silver is created from hope,
The crash of impending bodies.

My beloved is mine. A train engine
Out of control, brakes pushed to floor.

Far from the Road

At the corner of Bluelick and North West,
Men and women disappear into night,
Shiver and sleep, dreaming on mattresses'

Blue ticking and stains.
This is how I imagined them. And this is how
I saw them in the fields surrounding this place.

The men and maybe the women—
Did I know then there were women?—
Dressed the same. They kept

Far from the road. In summer's fields,
They grew beans and corn.
They bent over the hoes in their hands,

One long rope of body under sun or oncoming storm.
They moved inside the heat like a single pearl
I'd seen on television, dropped into

That bottle of thick and sickeningly green shampoo.
I saw them only seconds, every day,
In their place. I saw them

From the backseat of my family's Bel-Air wagon.
We were on our way to go swimming,
Springbrook Swim Club,

Its pool above ground, oval cloud,
Haloed in pink and green neon
We could see from where the roads came together

A field's length away. The pool rose above that field
Like a heaven with cement guardrail
And streetlights posted all the way around.

Did my folks tell me anything as we passed
To make me feel sad or afraid?
Or did I simply see

The men on horseback also in those fields,
Rifles balanced across their laps,
And farther a fence taller than July's corn,

Outside walls of schoolhouse brick,
Older and plainer than a farmwife's face,
Thicker than the length of a husband's arm?

No one I knew had ever been inside that fence,
Inside those walls, so forget all about it,
My folks said, as soon as our car hit the pool's gravel lot,

As soon as our tires parked on loose stones.

II

My Name Is Quinn Margaret

My sister wore a peignoir
From the time she was three. She knew
All the names for froufrou nightgowns
And the time of night when any woman,
As she said, who was truly a woman,
Puts up her hair. Lucy Electa was nylon
On the move, hair spray and cherry-
Painted toes hitching roads
Named Bluelick and Slabtown.

When I was born, summer curled
Tomato leaves dead brown.
I was named Quinn, after a man,
My father's Indiana uncle who wasn't a man,
Really. He brought carnations
And pictures of his second house in Mexico,
Always the parrots and young boys
Whose names I couldn't say.

I was born with weevils in my stomach.
I was born with wooden feet,
Or, as my mother says, pronating arches.
My legs knocked. She says
My job is harder,
To be smart instead of beautiful,
To know men like Nietzsche,
Words in which women like my mother
Find inspiration: *that storm*
Which does not kill you makes you happier.

So each day I work harder,
My pink hands pulling

The strings that make my bottom half go.
I learn the names for my puppet parts:
Pelvis, a basin, *knee*, which is the joint
Between the thigh and lower leg. *Heel*,
Back part, despicable person.
The *foot*, a group of syllables
Serving as a unit of measure in verse.

I walk a slant board.
I pick up marbles with my toes.
My hands work faster. My legs faster,
Get strong, get hungry,
These parts below my stomach,
The sounds they make:
Wood against wood, Ohio Blue Tips,
And their harder job: *to burn*,
As in the verb, to be on fire.

Photograph: Xenia, 1979

Two children without sweaters
Stand on the backdoor stoop,
Screen door banging behind them.
A blond cat rubs against their legs,
The pumpkin-colored leggings and leaves.
Witches in black paper defend the windows,
Cover broken panes with their skirts.

The houses of our childhood,
Both of them, have burned down.
Barefoot, we forgot our shoes,
Forgot to walk them back out of the house.

Dollhouse

The white clapboard frame stands
For a man now dead with a wife
And their plans for this house.
The wife sits with a girl,
Grandchild beside the cat, curling
Tail against its haunches.
Her hair is white, color of cat,
And falls off her shoulders
The way sides of this house hinge open
In an insistent child's fingers.

She remembers out loud
A spinet piano and lilac details
Enacted now with clothespin dolls
In her old woman's hands.
A china cat, blond and black,
Sleeps in a wicker basket by the door.

The open door waits for a father
To step back into his wife's painted arms.
She knows how these walls
Fall away to contain the night
Where he hides. The yellow eyes
Of a cat fill the dollhouse windows.

Quinn Margaret, Who Still Lives at Home, Gets a Call from Lucy Electa, Her Sister, Now an Auto Show Girl

She asks, have I seen her?
There are billboards of her
All over Detroit.
She calls to say
That she, Lucy Electa,
Is an auto show girl.
She says it's hard work,
That she can't wear her glasses.
The carousels, turning,
Those sedans and Coupe Devilles,
Give her a motion sickness
For which she takes pills.
She says she's following
In the footsteps of Rosamond Harland,
Last year's winner in the national
TV Model Spokeswoman's Talent Search.
From Rosamond, she says, she's learned
To wear a Kool-Aid smile,
A lamé dress,
To drape one arm
When describing a single
Special feature, two arms
For the whole showcase window.

Right now, she says, she's between jobs,
Staying with a friend in Lorain.
She was lying, she says,
On the couch this past Sunday
When the sudden desire
To call overwhelmed her.
She was reading a queer book.
Quinn, she says, in high school

That's what we called them—
You remember the kind?
There's a woman on the cover
With lots of dark hair.
She's falling out of her dress.
The man, holding her in his arms,
Knows just where to stand
So he can see all she's got.
Quinn, she says,
I've got a few things to tell you.
It's about the women and these showrooms.

A Piece of Her Dress

Aunt Ella-Elizabeth in yellow light,
Whore's-hair yellow light,
Rocks in a fat and shiny chair.
She's wrapped in backstitch—
A quilt, the names of her girlfriends
And the same date on each square.
Stupid girls. Goddam. 1856.

Aunt Ella-Elizabeth on a farm of chickens
With me, her sister's kid.
Some mornings I scrape an apple,
Push it white and sweet right into her mouth.
The apple, it just sits there.

Aunt Ella-Elizabeth, I say, move your goddam mouth.
Show me some teeth.
She pulls her gray lips back then
Like a laughing dog.

Ellen, your daddy called you, Ellen,
Rubbing his forehead. Hard and yellow.
Ellen, he called you
To marry your first cousin, Harmon Grant.

There in Medina, Ohio,
Each girl gave a piece of her dress.
You all sat on wicker chairs on the porch.
Like ladies from some Presbyterian church,
You sewed a quilt-top. Full-blown Tulips.

Ellen, cows without bells grazed
In your daddy's orchard by the main house.

Those girls passed right by the stinking cows
Walking home. They saw your daddy in the yard. They
    waved.
But Harmon Grant and those goddam girls
Stopped coming. Your sister, muttering like a chicken,
She finished the quilt.

Aunt Ella-Elizabeth, now in that chair,
Lips buttoned tight as a lady's boot,
I know it's the apples,
How you like the thick taste of them a long time against your
    teeth.

The Home Place

Uncle Ed steps through the doorway.
He bends, unties his shoes.
Eggs soak in a steel bucket.
He lines the drawer with *Capper's Weekly*,
Partially covers the first page with silverware.
Alongside a photo of Hitler's army chief,
Mrs. Zula Bennington writes: *The other evening*
I took my children to a picture show,
Willard, Jr., on one side of me, Roy on the other.
We seated ourselves quietly.
Ed fingers the snapshot of a girl: she straddles a fence,
Her calves thick and white in the sun.
Uncle Ed sleeps on the narrow bed. The full weight
And impression of his body walks back into his shoes.
It turns, passes a feather through his pipe,
Strikes a match on the door.

The Garden's Wife

Along the clay tennis courts
And carriage house,
A woman
Who is not a mother
Rides a tractor.
I call her
Helen of Troy.
She lights
A cigarette,
Then takes off
Her shirt,
Smoke rolling on air.
She wears a belt mark
Wide around her middle
Like the furrow
A plow makes. Wide,
The way my father kissed
Along the nape
Of her blouse,
Dragging footsteps
Along the hedgerow.

The Day Quinn Margaret Blamed for Everything

My sister in the closet,
Spite-faced after a second grade day
When no one called her Zsa-Zsa,
Her peignoir, as she called it,
Sifted by moths.

She knows she is less interesting
Than the outskirts of an Ohio town—
A water tower standing in a field
Spray-painted in red,
Shaking letters: *Pictures of Lily*
Made my life so wonderful.

Lily is the unlikely
Name of a farmer's daughter,
Unlikely words on a water tower:
Blue eye, summer door.

Tractors

Ronnie's the shortest guard in the state of Ohio
Where he is champion
And best kisser of Susan Ellen Haubner. I know.
She says my brother Ronnie kisses like he plays
Basketball, quick and hard. She says he palms her ass
One-handed. She says Ronnie moves
Between her legs as if the whole state of Indiana and its governor
Came out to see how the game is played.
Ronnie goes with a girl who can talk like that.

Ronnie calls me Einstein. I say
Umbilicus for belly button.
Bowel movement for, you know. Ronnie says,
You can't make Einstein say shit.
On the way to the game Saturday night,
The family rides in a Bel-Air station wagon,
Ronnie rides with the team. In the back of the car,
I read *Webster's Dictionary*, find
One strong word for each letter in the rival team's name:

Bungarum, venomous snake from India
Without a hood. *Ubiquitous*, existing everywhere.
Levirate, the code of Moses: the dead man's brother
Must marry the widow if there are no sons.
Languette, insect tongue. *Slocking stone*,
Rich ore luring investors into a worthless mine.

So, tonight, the Bulls will be stronger.
In the back seat of the car Ronnie will borrow
After the game, Susan Ellen Haubner will say
Basketball players have no future.
She will dump Ronnie

For Coach Jackson's son who has, as she says,
The fine, steady hands of a surgeon.

I don't know what I want. But when the crowd
Jumps to its feet, last thirty seconds,
They roar like the engines. They are all
The tractors in Ohio.

Almanac

Back then, I knew what I liked:
Tomatoes huddled in hothouses,
The fat, splitting red
Faces of German gardeners.
The Loeschers
Sold the hothouses to the bank.
Bill Loescher, the grandson, the heir,
The first boy in our school
To drink coffee and eat shrimp in a restaurant.
The first boy. Back then,
Hawthorns and marigolds
Grew on Sugar Street.
Blisters bubbled the bottoms of my feet.
The pool swam against them,
Sandpaper on soft wood.
I liked the bleeding,
Rubbing my raw toes against
The also-raw toes of my favorite boy—
Cousin Brian—
Not the one everyone thought.
I liked that my desire was a secret:
A criminal's herb
Fundamental and growing,
The bone twitch in a girl's hip,
Summer squash that in one day
Outgrows the garden
But not summer—
Big, but not the whole season.
Back then, I liked calves,
Young cows and the legs
On a left-handed girl.
They stood straight and strong.

I liked sweat,
Its coral-vine
Trails along my baked skin.
I liked that Wednesday was the hungriest
Day in the middle
Of abandon and houseflies.
I liked a thunderstorm's electric dirt,
The way it started the dog.
Back then, I liked
That sometimes penniless sky.

The First Good Day of My Life

The sun was a girl.
She was the blue light,
Aegean Sea,
I once saw in a travel book.
The sun was blue through the draperies,
Then yellow as its small feet
Crept into the room.
She was a girl who knew
She didn't want to get caught.
In a house for the twitterpated:
Lilacs on the side
And wood violets under the elms.

I am a woman with jawbreakers in my pocket.
I wear one of many navy-colored T-shirts
I've collected from local fire departments.
These shirts are my signature.

I knew her the moment I saw her,
That sun like a secret pen pal
You finally get to meet.
I was sprawled out
With my baby bottle of peach juice.
I was too old for that bottle,
Too big to hide like I used to
Under the drop leaf table.
I swore that sun,
Who dangled her skinny legs over the sill,
That sun winked at me.

I swear.
I live in the desert

Where I grow hibiscus in pots.
I tack postcards over my desk:
Ché Guevara, Donald Sutherland,
And Mary Steenbergen in a black strapless dress.
They help me visualize what I want.
One is a picture of three women.
They feed goldfish in a marble pool—
Silver Favourites *by Sir Lawrence Alma-Tadema.*
Behind the pool is the Aegean.

Uncle Brad was not really my uncle.
He stood in the doorway.
He held a beer and a cigarette.
I wondered how long he had been here.
I wondered if he would tell my parents what he saw.
The sun stayed right where she was,
Stayed still without flinching.
I took my cue from her.

I grow wood violets, too,
Hyacinth and Martha Washington red geraniums.
The sun in the afternoon yard is strange.
She never stays long.
This weekend I'm moving my father out of his house.
My friend Laurie has a truck.
She says we can do it ourselves,
A dolly and planks.
We don't need to call strapping men.
Laurie is a sculptor.
She works with metal, running water, and plants.
I will buy her a wrist corsage
For her opening at the Ice House.

I could not tell him,
Uncle Brad, who took me out on his boat
In Lake St. Mary's hard water.
I could not tell him I was scared.

He smiled at me funnylike.
He told me St. Mary's was a manmade lake.
A wind on a lake that shallow was more dangerous.
I smiled back. The sun was high and behind me.
This was the first good day of my life.

Small Oceans

Love's error in water

—Robert Creeley

Afternoon, blue
In a sun caught entering our kitchen window,
Its cotton half-curtain. Let me start again.

Afternoon, damp
Walls of the summer house. Azure-like blanket.
We lie, the sides of this ship a cradle.

Outside, the beaches. Sailors' faces lit up,
Shaking. Open the window.
Their gull-like cries over the immovable body.

I want you. I want you.
This sea enters your footprints
Like an offering to a sexual Jesus.

Hair in Jean Harlow waves,
A cargo of pearls. I'm golden. I'm wet.
This is what I meant to say.

This Summer That Isn't Mine

He was the one I saw
Who caught the tired dog, paddling
Tough water behind the boat. I still see him.

He was my uncle, the ropes of his arms
The dog gave himself to.
A boat on hard water,

Wind kicking in, he drank beer,
Black Label, sang Motown—
Ain't Nothin' Like the Real Thing—

Arc of the sail, whip and snap
Like a locker-room towel on the back of a thigh.
This was a pain, quick and beautiful,

Slipknot through a brass ring. When you pull
Just so, like that, it lets go, easylike,
You know, just like I showed you.

But it is my ankle that cuts the water,
You see, my foot dangling,
Summer fish, for the first time,

Pulling up and away from the side of this boat.
You are my uncle, my cousin's father,
Twelve years older than me with a T-shirt waving

From the back of your jeans like an armada's flag.
This summer that isn't mine
Swims away hungry on St. Mary's Lake.

And it stays with you,
Smell of sun oil and sweat.
The water of the fish's eye is cold and pure,

The way it swims right through you.
Nearly drowned, the dog sleeps at my uncle's feet,
Your feet, and you ease the boat back in,

Ask me did I have a good time,
Then, just like you were forgetting something,
Ask me do I want to take the boat out again.

Schoonover's Lake

A face with sunlight
6:00 P.M.
And suppertime
Silver green
Sea foam green
The lake with willowy trees
Isadora Duncan willows
Dipping their hair in sunlight
A woman's face with lakelight
Catching the lake
Holding the light
Fireflies of first evening
The lake with moss
The lake with water spiders
Small imperfections
On a face with sunlight
Honey light on your face
The lake's eyes
Brown bottomless eyes
Swimming with gold fishes
Feeding the fishes
Feeding the lake's mouth
A face already full of sunlight
Bread from my own face
Covering the lake with kisses

Staying Dressed

Your voice in the doorway
Full with handknit sweaters,
A scarf, the purple wool.

Your voice in the room
Removes a coat,
Sits, crosses
One leg over the other.
Your voice unties a shoe.

Your voice after dinner
Folds a napkin, runs
Steaming water for dishes,
Rolls up a sleeve.

In bed, it pulls back
The covers, stretches
Blond with a cat. Nude,
It crawls to my mouth.

My Father's Horses

I see them everywhere,
And my dumb lips like thin snails
Trail over their own shimmering,
Wet. I see them,
And my lips are the felt wrappings tied twice
Around the legs of an oak table.
Their heads in blue light.
I see them with their nostrils,
Chins tucked into chest,
Into the black armoire,
The beautiful brass latchings.
I see them from a window—
The carrots boiling there below
Raise their rough steam
Like the stableman's two hands.
These are the horses of summer lunches.
The knotted, now unbraidable hair in its dust
And McCrery's Cream Cheese in a plain brown box.
I see they are actors.
Imported from Sweden,
They read the dark Neruda in blond sweaters.
I fall from their laughter,
Lips pulled back from teeth.
I would race them to be naked,
Pull the black sweater
Off over my head,
My invisible haunches quivering.

The Eccentric Beauty

I collect snails
At night,
Set out grapefruits,
Half-moon traps
Hollowed out.
The snails
Are gray lips
Over these breasts.
They push small circles
Of brown earth.
By morning,
The fruit is full
With their bodies.

The house
Has no floorboards,
Only pots of geraniums,
Wicker furniture
Untroubled
As our small town,
Which doesn't wander
Far down its road.

My father
In a new linen suit
Is Satie's beauty,
A gardener
Pruning camellias.
His cordovan loafers
Are caked with mud,
And under his nails
Bits of garden stay.

Well-trained butlers,
The trees
Accept his shirt.
They nod their heads.
It is their nature,
It is summer, they say,
When night girls
Open their windows.

III

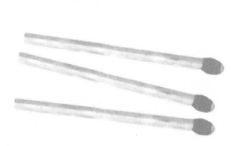

I, Quinn Margaret, Take You

> *The lower jaw of a horse, so joined to an oak*
> *branch that no traces of its insertion remain.*
>
> —Ole Worm, 1649

What is the bone?
A tree
In a horse's head.
What is the bone
Of desire?
A horse's head
In a tree.

An upper lip
Full of summer apples,
Tart, the squeeze
And drip after a swim
In Schoonover's pond.
I eat the apples,
Pucker my lip.
I throw their cores
Against the tree.

On this hillside,
I am away
For a moment
From the blue drawing room
Where your mother
Plans our marriage.
Chin propped against knuckles,
My jaw aches.
Magritte's red lips
Pressed together

Are the legs on a long woman,
Part in a sky
Of fat clouds.
The clouds
Rattle against me, teacups.
They are your women.
They crack,
Climb dripping back

Into the cupboard,
Their sticky rings.
Tonight these women
Will be all your wives.
My jaw now is a letter.
Its pretty envelopes open
In the small hours of the night.
This stops me.

You make the sound
Of a toy bugle.
Your words march over
The blanket:
Eat the cake,
I pretend you say,
The soft undercooked insides
Where it is sweet and good.
The pralines.

Eat the fat sandwich
In its white bun,
The stringy corned beef,
The butter.
Eat me with a lettuce,
My porridge
On the end of a spoon.

Kitchen Matches

Some women can reconstruct the body
From a single organ. Take the hand.
Like children, they play connect the dots
With the hand's eighteen numbers,
Trace to nineteen up the back of an arm.
Twenty, twenty-one, the face.
They light with a match each black dot,
Numbers burning then a luminous blue.

I have never been naked.
Dressed in cotton nightdresses,
I read about the Greeks who plunge
Headfirst into the Aegean.
I have never been that angry.
Singsong. Little ditties.
I bite the inside of my own red mouth.

This anger is no anger.
The back muscles, knees.
My own steel hand. Naked, now,
I sit on the wooden chair.
You walk around me,
Kindly think to cover me,
To light, as if with a match,
This blue arm.

The Child Swinging between Their Hands

Her husband sits by
When on Thursdays
She shaves.
Her legs, she says,
Are twins.
They are the maples
She used as a girl
To fashion kites.
They are weighted
As she remembers
With pond water
And orange fishes.

She remembers her dress
The summer she jumped
Free of it,
Then stepped back
Into the lake.
Her bare back, she says,
Felt like sky.

She says she swam
Like the black dog
That returned to her,
A wet bird in its mouth.
Two sisters walked by,
Hands deep
In their navy pockets.

I thought of them
Going home, she says,

Taking a bath.
One slides
A bar of soap.
The other one falls.
Two hands. Unbelieveable sisters.

Making a Marriage from Scratch

Stop slittering,
Quinn Margaret's mother says.
Her mother's eyes
Are the dumb brown of potatoes,
Rolling boil
In her hot-water face.
She scrapes carrots
Into a bucket, the skinny peels.
She will make them soup.
Yellow rutabagas,
The mutton bone,
Rough soup with griddle scones.

Quinn Margaret collects
Those Moo-Cow Creamers.
She buys them at the Union 76.
She knows that like men
They will lower
Their flat, white cheeks.
She knows men's lips
Are full, call *forevermore*—
Their lips that loosen
Red boats.
She knows the men
Lick their fingers,
That taste of barley-sugar
Animals on a stick.

Quinn Margaret collects
Antique eggbeaters.
She collects flagstone
Porch steps and sweeper parts.
She lines sprinkler heads

Along the garage wall.
These she buys new.
She knows that marriage smell:
Iced tea with lemon,
Charcoal briquets.

Quinn Margaret always forgets
Where the fork goes.
Left-handed,
She sets the table backwards,
Steams glasses
With her breath,
Wipes the rims
With her shirtsleeve.
And with her eyes closed,
Her hand on the cane back,
She forgets where to put
Her husband's chair.

Trimble Jackson calls himself
A caulk chiseler.
He makes his way
Stripping tiles
In showers and tubs.
He works
For The Tornado Company.
In summer,
He hates his job.
The thermals and rain
Are cows calling.
Grass is the slight hair
He presses into his face.
Grass is the first smell
Of summer's cut and rake.

Trimble Jackson bought
A blue-eyed calf.

It's deaf
Like those white cats
That can hear
Only when their eyes
Are turned orange.
In a hand-colored photograph,
The calf stands still.
Trimble Jackson stands
Ten years in front of it.

Trimble Jackson's wife
Makes a sweater. Quinn Margaret,
Still on needles, unravels
As far as the door,
As far as he comes
To bring her some forsythia
Or clatter home
To ask
For a cheese sandwich.

Trimble Jackson doesn't know
What to do
With Quinn Margaret's mother's cats.
They are all white or blond.
Mae West cats,
They drink the water
From bowls of pansies.
They knock the flower stems out,
Leave spots
On the eyelet tableskirts.
Trimble Jackson's hands
Touch the scrubbed floors
Where the cats sleep
And where lemon oil
On a torn pajama
Should be a wife's job.

Drawing a House

I've got this big piece of paper,
Stretch it across my belly.
I'm thinking of how
The smell of fields
Enters a house.
Touched by lightning,
It is opened,
Hot zipper,
Blackened pants whistling.

I'm thinking of what
Is ordinary: a couple,
A windowpane,
Maybe a Martha Washington
Red geranium.
They meet by chance.
They'll always be here.

I'm thinking of when
A troubled boat
Is blue
As this house,
As my belly burning,
Turning silver,
Turning to ash
And quiet rumbling.
It's too late
To ask
What happened
At the beginning.

Summer Fruit

The houses push
Against each other,
Their fight
In tug-of-war clotheslines.
The women string
Their clothes on rope.
In summer,
They fasten socks
And underthings
With wooden pins
Close together.
The wooden pins
Are the kind
Their daughters use
To make dolls
To play
In shoebox houses.
Folded laundry
Is a map
Of this town.

The women hook
Beaded necklaces
Behind their necks.
The beads, they think,
Are pearl-sized words,
The words
They can't say.
They hang
Close to each other.
Summer's fruit,
They are

The dessert grapes, frozen
And dusted with sugar,
Jonathan apples,
Quince, wild cherries,
The Carmen Miranda bananas.
The women look
From their kitchen windows.
They see
Their wild-eyed laundry
Watching them.
It's summer,
They take it in.

Everything about Men

The cat watched
While I did it:
Flat on the floor,
An angel spread out,
Fallen naked,
Passed over.
Black thong,
Woolen tam and socks
Worn for protection,
Color of oatmeal,
In need of a wash.
I light a familiar fire.
Blue gaslight
Flames under a saucepan,
Dancing blue mouths
And eyelids.
Steam rises
From a cast-iron pot,
Boiling meat
And onions.

Quinn Margaret Likes to Cook

Quinn Margaret is shy with the butcher.
She buys chickens prepackaged,
Bones them with her own fingers,
Flattens them with the knife's dull edge.
Quinn Margaret likes this man,
Who has a bell on the counter.
She could touch that bell lightly twice
And he'd come out from the back.
Hands in a white cotton towel,
He'd ask if she needs anything.
Quinn Margaret can't make her fingers
Do something that simple.
Even a small bell is loud,
Is church,
That call that says, Hurry,
Scones are done baking.
Quinn Margaret cuts them from dough
The size of the juice glass
Passed down from Grandmother Blanton,
Its painted oranges and leaves,
Green, the perfect O of its lip.
Quinn Margaret likes to cook,
She likes the leftover dough
After the cutting.
The way it looks pocked
Reminds her of the butcher's face.
She squeezes it in her hands
Like a sweet orange instead of bread
Or like an orange-flavored bread,
Yes, she thinks,
Where the tastes mingle.
These raisined biscuits,

Full with walnuts and zest,
Sour milk and soda,
Dusted with flour,
She takes them from the oven.
This is what she can imagine:
These scones on a plate,
Quinn Margaret leaving them
On the glass-topped counter
Next to the bell
Mouth that opens.

Going Back Home

Doors swell shut this time of year.
Mold grows around their frames
Like the five-o'clock shadow on a husband's face.
I left him just that way.

My mother, who has a scripture for everything,
Says the Book of Philemon speaks of my husband
As parted from me for a season,
That I should have him back forever,

Both in the flesh and in the Lord.
She says I'm like the Easter storm in '65
Ripping up whole families by the roots.
Elm Street becomes Market.

The Presbyterians go downtown,
A wreckage of windows and clapboard.

The Serving of a Good Aunt

A shepherdess hidden on the porcelain plate
Is a map forgotten by geographers,

Beads of paint on an invisible thread.
In this room, a red brow turns

Under stick bone fingers:
Aunt Leona Mae's brambled hair, an extravagance

Like electrical wires made of copper,
Winter violets, and white batiste nightdress.

She fills the porcelain plate
With scones, pours black tea:

Sheep, noses to the ground, and a shepherdess,
Dead branch over the river.

How Quinn Margaret Fights

See, the dust storm is coming,
Only not romantic with stories,
Red and satin lips that pillow.

She said, *if I weren't a lady* . . .
Opening and closing her mouth like a fish,
She steps into the rain,

A sound like *blue* or *you* climbing
Hand over hand inside her chest.
In a back room and under the bed, a dog whines.

If only you would touch my face,
She says, comfortless, in mid-ocean,
Dreaming of fish in place of eyes.

The Music Night Plays

Small trees
Begin to shimmer.
Nothing walks away
Or returns.
No one stays for supper.

The hawthorn uprooted
In the park
Is a rough arm
Ripped from its origin,
Its fingers pressing
Against the ground.
It is the black
After-fire
Of a woman.

She braids back her hair.
Night can no longer
Surprise her
With its long walk,
Its tails shining
Up the stairway.
She hears music,
Which is
Its own skin.

The Each Day Women

The oldest among them comes closer,
Dances down wooden steps,

Dances with us in the full room
Where night has unraveled her hair.

And this one now in front of us,
With her terrible feet hammering,

Unwrapped and unburied,
Into winter's sunlight takes everything.

She works the ceiling,
The seams between floorboards.

She will take us outside,
Let go of our fingers,

Unstring the calves of her legs.
She will dance herself up the short stairs.

Always it is as if she is already gone.
Always she is dressed to go:

An overcoat and felt hat on the outside,
And on the inside, old husbands and mice.

The Haw Is the Berry

I am frightened
To boil fish,
To set a good table:
The fish eyes
Shine back at me.
Still, I do as I'm told.

One summer,
My father,
Walking the park,
Took a thorn
From a boy's foot.
He worked it slow
Between his fingers
The way he took
An apple
From a small pocket.

I walk the same park.
When fields are summer,
My father takes me back.
Touch the iris, the wood violets,
Straw hats, he says,
They are the color of crickets
And spiders.
This is the way
What is invisible becomes his:
Rising bread,
The hard wood
Of English hawthorn.

What Bread Isn't and Is

This bread is not food,
Not slices perfectly salted with salmon,
Not Norway or Scotland who ship this fish.

It is not origin or home or place,
Kneaded and pressed, recalled like a smell
That rises from afternoon's kitchen.

This bread is not body. Not even a man,
Joe Silver, his dough-white belly
Or cream spilling on his coffee-stained pants.

This bread is not stupid,
Not fresh or young like flowers,
Not summer confused with geraniums.

It is not Sugar Street
Lined with elms and tricycles,
Their bent bones limp and forgiving.

This bread that I take
Is not the Jones's backyard, is not an arm's reach
To the cherries that grew there.

This bread is not and is more
Than a trembling climb up the soft trunk,
The strike of a fall, digits making

Their five ways back along ground—earth's bowl—
Scraping the tree's zest, its skin
Bark that is not lemon or spice.

This bread is not only what the fingers can make—
Braided basket and splintering eggshell—
But something of what they can reach and remember:

Rumorous branch,
Yolk that is eye and breast and tongue,
The hen's faithful laying.

It is the neighborhood's houses,
Corrugated boxes,
The crumbs' sweet prayer.

Bells, She Hears

A woman before bed
Puts her two shoes
Side by side,
Forgets the stairway light.
She scrubs her skin
With calendula soap,
Washes away salt
And the fish and garlic
Of her hands.

She tells her hands
To make noise,
Tells them, Applaud.
This is my work,
She says, and this work
Is a new dress.

Her boy, small
Inside her,
Grinning and toothless,
Listens to the men and women,
Keeps something
For himself:
The carnation smell
At the nape of her neck.

Everything is changing
Into her,
Into a plowed field
Into brown shoes
Her body when wind
Lifts her dress.

That Summer, Joe, and Prison

1

Ohio, with its steel-toed boots,
Heels worn away on the outside.
These boots are shackled
Like a chain of Coniber traps;
Ankles, the twice-sprung necks of muskrat.
Gray day workclothes hang
From window bars by a rope.
Ohio, an inmate's sucker-punched face,
Peony face, swollen
And latticed with ants,
Its broken nose bleeding from one side.
Ohio's wrists are leashed
By leather, its puppet hands
Playing to a full house. Wooden heads
Jerking off on a day-hall rug.

Ohio then, with its petticoat sail
Skirting the lake. Bare-breasted,
Bikini top whipping a mast,
Its tin bucket full
Of bluegills dropped back.
Ohio on holiday,
Tongue licking colored ice,
A thin-wristed lover,
Sunburned and sleeping,
Its fingers, a ribboned ponytail
Twisting down the back,
Fingers that loose a rope from the pier.
Ohio, a four-pointed star
Spread out under moonlight,

Its pretty ankles
Dipping the green water.

2

Ohio, wrist under the hand of Michigan,
Riot gear stacked in hallways,
The Man figures my worth
As a hostage: young, white teacher—
Single female, with child. I'm worth too much.
He sends me home for the weekend.
Johnny Crusoe sends each pitch
Home, over the wall. Crash Redell
Glides his face through plate glass.
The Man cancels passes, fishing.
And you, slamming a ball down the alley,
Break the pinsetter's leg at the knee.

Bluegills in a tin bucket,
And the man I've invited from New York
Dangles his chicken-bone wrist
Over the side of the boat. I float on my back,
Casting into night: boathouse dinner,
Then the moon, shiver of glass,
Spreads out on the deck.

The Man called you Fat-Boy-in-Trouble, Joe,
Strapped you four ways down to a Marlowe bed,
Bread-dough belly breathing hard,
Rising naked and fast in 102 degrees,
Six-by-eight room. You called for water.
And sometime before morning,
The man from New York pissed
From the side of the boat. It was summer,
And laughing and good. The trouble, Joe,
Falling back and away from me.

Notes

"Reckoning" is dedicated to Michael Smith, 1937-89.

"On His Sixteenth Birthday, His Mother Calls the Season" is for Laura Lee.

"The House Next Door" is for Noah Sweeney.

"The Game Joe Silver Plays Alone and in the Dark" draws on a painting by Leon Waller.

"A Day for Fishing" refers to Marlowe beds, which are beds that have slatted headboards and footboards shaped like upsidedown *U*'s. They appear frequently in posh furniture catalogues, but bolted to the floor in a prison ward, they work efficiently for restraining inmates.

"On the Day before Joe Silver Was Made" adapts several lines from the Song of Songs.

"The Home Place" draws on a photograph by Wright Morris.

"Almanac" is for Theresa.

"Schoonover's Lake" is for Crista.

"The Serving of a Good Aunt" draws on a line from *Wind, Sand, and Stars* by Antoine de St. Exupery.

"That Summer, Joe, and Prison" refers to a practice in some prisons where officials assign hostage value numbers to employees. The number indicates an employee's hostage value to inmates in the event of a riot. Value goes up in proportion to the likelihood the administration would negotiate for a particular employee's release.

About the Author

Jeanne E. Clark was born and raised in northwest Ohio. She teaches creative writing at Arizona State University and for the Arizona Commission on the Arts as an Artist-in-Education. She was the winner of the 1995 Loft Prize in Poetry.

About the Book

This book was set in a digitized version of Dante.
Composed by Septima Designs, Athens, Ohio
Printed and bound by Thomson Shore, Inc., Dexter, Michigan
Design by Chiquita Babb